- *Certification of TS16949 IN HOBEL BELLOWS IN THE YEAR 2012*
- *Ensured compliance of customer delivery schedule by controlling parts*
- *production cycle.*
- *Rejection control ----Achieved rejection percentage <1 ,50 ppm for process*
- *and supplier Year2013*

INTRODUCTION

Seven basic tools of quality, first emphasized by Kaoru Ishikawa, a professor of engineering at Tokyo University and the father of "quality circles." These tools are as given as below –

1. <u>Cause-and-effect diagram</u> (also called Ishikawa or fishbone chart):
2. Identifies many possible causes for an effect or problem and sorts ideas into useful categories.
3. <u>Check sheet:</u> A structured, prepared form for collecting and analyzing

data; a generic tool that can be adapted for a wide variety of purposes.

4. Control charts: Graphs used to study how a process changes over time.

5. Histogram: The most commonly used graph for showing frequency

or how often each different value in a set of data occurs.

6. Pareto chart: Shows on a bar graph which factors are more significant.

7. Scatter diagram: Graphs pairs of numerical data, one variable on each

axis, to look for a relationship.

7 Flow chart: A process flow chart is simply a tool that graphically shows

the inputs, actions, and outputs of a given system

8 Drive,

9 Process mapping,

10 Brain storming

11 Force field analysis

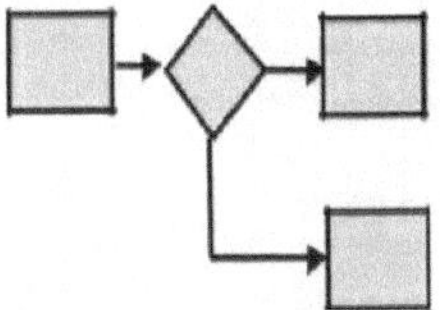

Effect Diagrams

Cause-

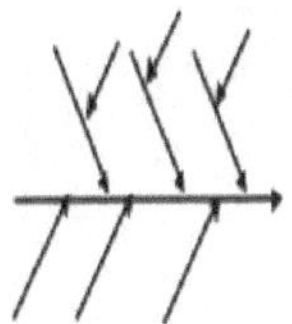

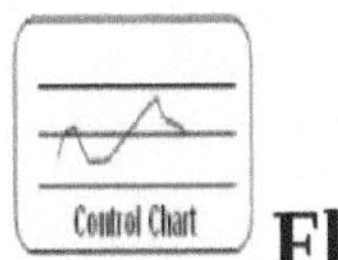

Flow Charts

Tools

Histogram Drive,process mapping,

Pareto chart,Force field analysis

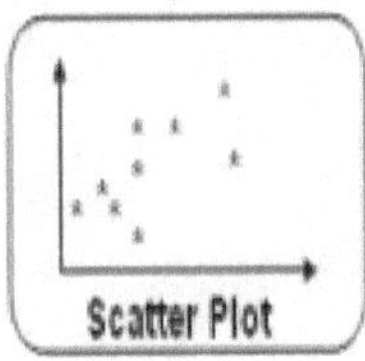

Where did the Basic Seven come from?

Kaoru Ishikawa

- Known for " Democratizing Statistics "

- The Basic Seven Tools made statistical analysis less complicated for the average person

Good Visual Aids make statistical and quality control more comprehendible

CAUSE AND EFFECT DIAGRAMS

Process improvement involves taking action on the causes of variation. With most practical applications, the number of possible causes for any given problem can be huge. Dr. Kaoru Ishikawa developed a simple method of graphically displaying the causes of any given quality problem. His method is called by several names, the Ishikawa diagram, the fishbone diagram, and the cause and effect diagram.

Cause and effect diagrams are tools that are used to organize and graphically display all of the knowledge a group has relating to a particular problem. Usually, the steps are the following:

1. Develop a flow chart of the area to be improved.

2. Define the problem to be solved.

3. Brainstorm to find all possible causes of the problem.

4. Organize the brainstorming results in rational categories.

5. Construct a cause and effect diagram that accurately displays the relationships of all the data in each category.

Once these steps are complete, constructing the cause and effect diagram is very simple.

1. Draw a box on the far right-hand side of a large sheet of paper and draw a horizontal arrow that points to the box. Inside of the box, write the description of the problem you are trying to solve.

2. Write the names of the categories above and below the horizontal line. Think of these as branches from the main trunk of the tree.

3. Draw in the detailed cause data for each category. Think of these as limbs and twigs on the branches.

A good cause and effect diagram will have many "twigs,".If your cause and effect diagram doesn't have a lot of smaller branches and twigs, it shows that the understanding of the problem is superficial. Chances are you need the help of someone outside of your group to aid in the understanding, perhaps someone more closely associated with the problem.

Cause and effect diagrams come in several basic types. The dispersion analysis type is created by repeatedly asking "why does this dispersion occur?" For example, we might want to know why all of our fresh peaches don't have the same color.

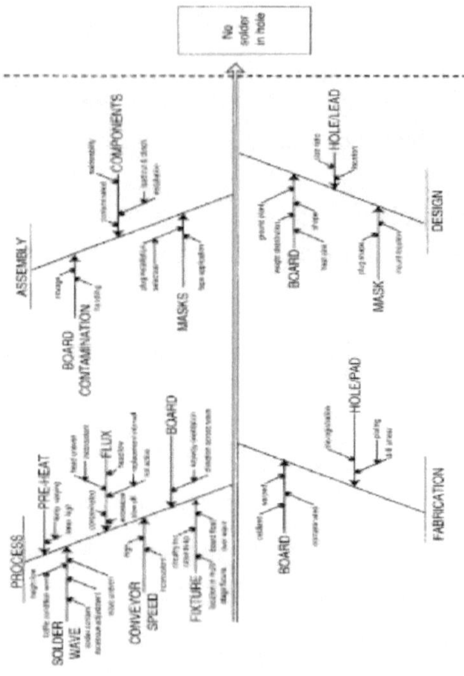

Cause and Effect diagram

The production process class cause and effect diagram uses production processes as the main categories, or branches, of the diagram. The cause enumeration cause and effect diagram simply displays all possible causes of a given problem grouped a

ccording to rational categories. This type of cause and effect diagram lends itself readily to the brainstorming approach we are using. Cause and effect diagrams have a number of uses. Creating the diagram is an education in itself. Organizing the knowledge of the group serves as a guide for discussion and frequently inspires more ideas. The cause and effect diagram, once created, acts as a record of your research. Simply record your tests and results as you proceed. If the true cause is found to be something that wasn't on the original diagram, write it in. Finally, the cause and effect diagram is a display of your current level of understanding. It shows the existing level of technology as understood by the team. It is a good idea to post the cause and effect diagram in a prominent location for all to see.

CHECK SHEETS

Check sheets are devices which consist of lists of items and some indicator of how often each item on the list occurs. In their simplest form, checklists are tools that make the data collection process easier by providing pre-written descriptions of events likely to occur. A well-designed check sheet will answer the questions posed by the investigator. Some examples of questions are the following: "Has everything been done?" "Have all inspections been performed?" "How often does a particular problem occur?" "Are problems more common with part X than with part Y?" They also serve as reminders that direct the attention of the data collector to items of interest and importance. Such simple check sheets are called confirmation check sheets. Check sheets have been improved by adding a number of enhancements, a few of which are described below. Although they are simple, check sheets are extremely useful process-improvement and problem-solving tools. Their power is greatly enhanced when they are used in conjunction with other simple tools, such as histograms and Pareto analysis. Ishikawa estimated that 80% to 90% of all workplace problems could be solved using only the simple quality improvement tools.

Check sheets are great tools for organizing and collecting facts and data. By collecting data, individuals or teams can make better decisions, solve problems faster, and earn management support.

Recording Check Sheets

A recording check sheet is used to collect measured or counted data. The simplest form of the recording check sheet is for counted data. Data is collected by making tick marks on this particular style of Check sheets

Errors	Days of Week						Total
	1	2	3	4	5	6	
Defective Pilot Light	卌 卌	卌	卌	卌 |||	卌 ||	卌	40
Loose Fasteners								卌	卌				16
Scratches			||	||			||	卌 卌	21
Missing Parts											3
Dirty Contacts	卌		|||	卌 ||	|||	卌	卌	32
Other			|||				||	|||	9
Total	19	19	16	19	23	25	121

Typical Recording Check Sheet

The check sheet can be broken down to indicate either shift, day, or month. Measured data may be summarized by the means of a check sheet called a tally sheet. To collect measured data, the same general check sheet form is used. The only precaution is to leave enough room to write in individual measurements.

Checklists

The second major type of check sheet is called the checklist. A grocery list is a common example of a checklist. On the job, checklists may often be used for inspecting machinery or product. Checklists are also very helpful when learning how to operate complex or delicate equipment.

Date: _______ Area _______	Visual Inspection	Washed once per Week	Supervisor (Operator)
Preheat House			
A2 Tub Room			
A3 Tub Room			
A Press Room			
B Press Room			
Finishing Room			
Roll Mill Room			

Process check sheets

These check sheets are used to create frequency distribution tally sheets that are, in turn, used to construct histograms. A process check sheet is constructed by listing several ranges of measurement values and recording a mark for the actual observations. Notice that if reasonable care is taken in recording tick marks, the check sheet gives a graphical picture similar to a histogram.

RANGE OF MEASUREMENTS	FREQUENCY
0.990-0.995 INCHES	////
0.995-1.000 INCHES	THL
1.001-1.005 INCHES	THL ////
1.006-1.010 INCHES	THL THL //
1.011-1.015 INCHES	////
1.016-1.020 INCHES	//

Process checklist

Defect check sheets

Here the different types of defects are listed and the observed frequencies observed. If reasonable care is taken in recording tick marks, the check sheet resembles a bar chart.

DEFECT	FREQUENCY
COLD SOLDER	////
NO SOLDER IN HOLE	THL THL ////
GRAINY SOLDER	THL ////
HOLE NOT PLATED THROUGH	THL THL ///
MASK NOT PROPERLY INSTALLED	THL ////
PAD LIFTED	/

Defect checklist

Stratified defects check sheets

These check sheets stratify a particular defect type according to logical criteria. This is helpful when the defect check sheet fails to provide adequate information regarding the root cause or causes of a problem.

SAMPLES OF 1,000 SOLDER JOINTS	PART NUMBER X-1011	PART NUMBER X-2011	PART NUMBER X-3011	PART NUMBER X-4011	PART NUMBER X-5011
COLD SOLDER	////			THL	
NO SOLDER IN HOLE	THL		//	//	
GRAINY SOLDER	THL	/		///	
HOLE NOT PLATED THROUGH	THL			///	
MASK NOT PROPERLY INSTALLED	THL		////	THL	
PAD LIFTED	/				

Stratified defect check sheet

Defect location check sheet

These "check sheets" are actually drawings, photographs, layout diagrams or maps
which show where a particular problem occurs. The spatial location is valuable in identifying root causes and planning corrective action. In the Figure below, the location of complaints from customers about lamination problems on a running shoe are shown with an "X." The diagram makes it easy to identify a problem area that would be difficult to depict otherwise. In this case, a picture is truly worth a thousand words of explanation.

Defect location check sheet lamination complaints.

Cause and effect diagram check sheet

Cause and effect diagrams can also serve as check sheets. Once the diagram has been prepared, it is posted in the work area and the appropriate arrow is marked whenever that particular cause or situation occurs. Teams can also use this approach for historic data, when such data is available.

HISTOGRAMS

A histogram is a pictorial representation of a set of data. It is created by grouping the measurements into "cells." Histograms are used to determine the shape of a data set. Also, a histogram displays the numbers in a way that makes it easy to see the dispersion and central tendency and to compare the distribution to requirements. Histograms can be valuable troubleshooting aids. Comparisons between histograms from different machines, operators, vendors, etc., often reveal important differences.

How to construct a histogram
1. Find the largest and the smallest value in the data.
2. Compute the range by subtracting the smallest value from the largest

value.

3. Select a number of cells for the histogram. Table below provides some useful guidelines. The final histogram may not have exactly the number of cells you choose here, as explained below. As an alternative, the number of cells can be found as the square root of the number in the sample. For example, if n=100, then the histogram would have 10 cells. Round to the nearest integer.

SAMPLE SIZE	NUMBER OF CELLS
100 or less	7 to 10
101-200	11 to 15
201 or more	16 to 20

4. Determine the width of each cell. We will use the letter W to stand for the cell width. The number W is a starting point. Round W to a convenient number. Rounding W will affect the number of cells in your histogram.

$$W = \frac{Range}{Number\ of\ Cells}$$

5. Compute "cell boundaries." A cell is a range of values and cell boundaries define the start and end of each cell. Cell boundaries should have one more decimal place than the raw data values in the data set. for example, if the data are integers, the cell boundaries would have one decimal place. The low boundary of the first cell must be less than the smallest value in the data set. Other cell boundaries are found
by adding W to the previous boundary. Continue until the upper boundary is larger than the largest value in the data set.

6. Go through the raw data and determine into which cell each value falls. Mark a tick in the appropriate cell.

7. Count the ticks in each cell and record the count, also called the frequency, to the right of the tick marks.

8. Construct a graph from the table. The vertical axis of the graph will show the frequency in each cell. The horizontal axis will show the cell boundaries. Figure below illustrates the layout of a histogram.

Layout of an histogram

9. Draw bars representing the cell frequencies. The bars should all be the same width, the height of the bars should equal the frequency in the cell.

Histogram example

Assume you have the data on the size of a metal rod. The rods were sampled every hour for 20 consecutive hours and 5 consecutive rods were checked each time.(20 subgroups of 5 values per group).

ROW	SAMPLE 1	SAMPLE 2	SAMPLE 3	SAMPLE 4	SAMPLE 5
1	1.002	0.995	1.000	1.002	1.005
2	1.000	0.997	1.007	0.992	0.995
3	0.997	1.013	1.001	0.985	1.002
4	0.990	1.008	1.005	0.994	1.012
5	0.992	1.012	1.005	0.985	1.006
6	1.000	1.002	1.006	1.007	0.993
7	0.984	0.994	0.998	1.006	1.002
8	0.987	0.994	1.002	0.997	1.008
9	0.992	0.988	1.015	0.987	1.006
10	0.994	0.990	0.991	1.002	0.988
11	1.007	1.008	0.990	1.001	0.999
12	0.995	0.989	0.982*	0.995	1.002
13	0.987	1.004	0.992	1.002	0.992
14	0.991	1.001	0.996	0.997	0.984
15	1.004	0.993	1.003	0.992	1.010
16	1.004	1.010	0.984	0.997	1.008
17	0.990	1.021*	0.995	0.987	0.989
18	1.003	0.992	0.992	0.990	1.014
19	1.000	0.985	1.019	1.002	0.986
20	0.996	0.984	1.005	1.016	1.012

1. Find the largest and the smallest value in the data set. The smallest value is 0.982 and the largest is 1.021.

2. Compute the range, R, by subtracting the smallest value from the largest value. R= 1.021 -0.982 = 0.039.

3. Select a number of cells for the histogram. Since we have 100 values, 7 to 10 cells are recommended. We will use 10 cells.

4. Determine the width of each cell, W. Using Equation V.I, we compute W=0.039 / 10 = 0.0039. We will round this to 0.004 for convenience. Thus, W= 0.004.

5. Compute the cell boundaries. The low boundary of the first cell must be

below our smallest value of 0.982, and our cell boundaries should have one decimal place more than our raw data. Thus, the lower cell boundary for the first cell will be 0.9815. Other cell boundaries are found by adding $W = 0.004$ to the previous cell boundary until the upper boundary is greater than our largest value of 1.021.

CELL NUMBER	LOWER CELL BOUNDARY	UPPER CELL BOUNDARY
1	0.9815	0.9855
2	0.9855	0.9895
3	0.9895	0.9935
4	0.9935	0.9975
5	0.9975	1.0015
6	1.0015	1.0055
7	1.0055	1.0095
8	1.0095	1.0135
9	1.0135	1.0175
10	1.0175	1.0215

6. Go through the raw data and mark a tick in the appropriate cell for each data point.

7. Count the tick marks in each cell and record the frequency to the right of each cell.

CELL NUMBER	CELL START	CELL END	TALLY	FREQUENCY
1	0.9815	0.9855	ЙΝ|||	8
2	0.9855	0.9895	ЙΝ||||	9
3	0.9895	0.9935	ЙΝЙΝЙΝ||	17
4	0.9935	0.9975	ЙΝЙΝЙΝ|	16
5	0.9975	1.0015	ЙΝ||||	9
6	1.0015	1.0055	ЙΝЙΝЙΝ||||	19
7	1.0055	1.0095	ЙΝЙΝ|	11
8	1.0095	1.0135	ЙΝ|	6
9	1.0135	1.0175	|||	3
10	1.0175	1.0215	||	2

Construct a graph from the above table. The frequency column will be plotted on the vertical axis, and the cell boundaries will be shown on the horizontal (bottom) axis. The resulting histogram is as shown

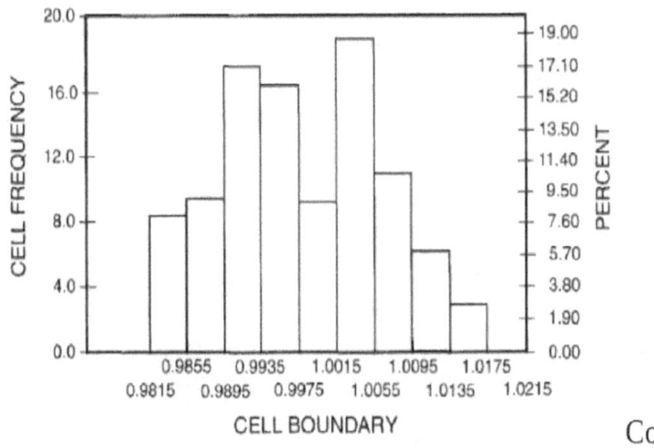

Completed Histogram

Use of Histogram

- Histograms can be used to compare a process to requirements if you draw the specification lines on the histogram. If you do this, be sure to scale the histogram accordingly.

- Histograms should not be used alone. Always construct a run chart or a control chart before constructing a histogram. They are needed because histograms will often conceal out of control conditions since they don't show the time sequence of the data.

- Evaluate the pattern of the histogram to determine if you can detect changes of any kind. The changes will usually be indicated by multiple modes or "peaks" on the histogram. Most real-world processes produce histograms with a single peak. However, histograms from small samples often have multiple peaks that merely represent sampling variation. Also, multiple peaks are sometimes caused by an unfortunate choice of the number of cells. Processes heavily influenced by behavior patterns are often multi-modal. For example, traffic patterns have distinct "rush-hours," and prime time is prime time precisely because more people tend to watch television at that time.

- Histograms can be used to compare a process to requirements if you draw the specification lines on the histogram. If you do this, be sure to scale the histogram accordingly.

- Histograms should not be used alone. Always construct a run chart or a control chart before constructing a histogram. They are needed because histograms will often conceal out of control conditions since they don't show the time sequence of the data.

- Evaluate the pattern of the histogram to determine if you can detect changes of any kind. The changes will usually be indicated by multiple modes or "peaks" on the histogram. Most real-world processes produce histograms with a single peak. However, histograms from small samples often have multiple peaks that merely represent sampling variation. Also, multiple peaks are sometimes caused by an unfortunate choice of the number of cells. Processes heavily influenced by behavior patterns are often multi-modal. For example, traffic patterns have distinct "rush-hours," and prime time is prime time precisely because more people tend to watch television at that time.

Histograms have the following characteristics:

- Frequency column graphs that display a static picture of process behavior. Histograms require a minimum of 50-100 data points.

- A histogram is characterized by the number of data points that fall within a given bar or interval. This is commonly referred to as "frequency."

- A stable process is frequently characterized by a histogram exhibiting unimodal or bell-shaped curves. A stable process is predictable.

- An unstable process is often characterized by a histogram that does exhibit a bell-shaped curve. Obviously other more exotic distribution shapes (like exponential, lognormal, gamma, beta, Weibull, Poisson, binomial, hypergeometric, geometric, etc.) exist as stable processes.

- When the bell curve is the approximate distribution shape, variation around the bell curve is chance or natural variation. Other variation is due to special or assignable causes.

Histogram Examples

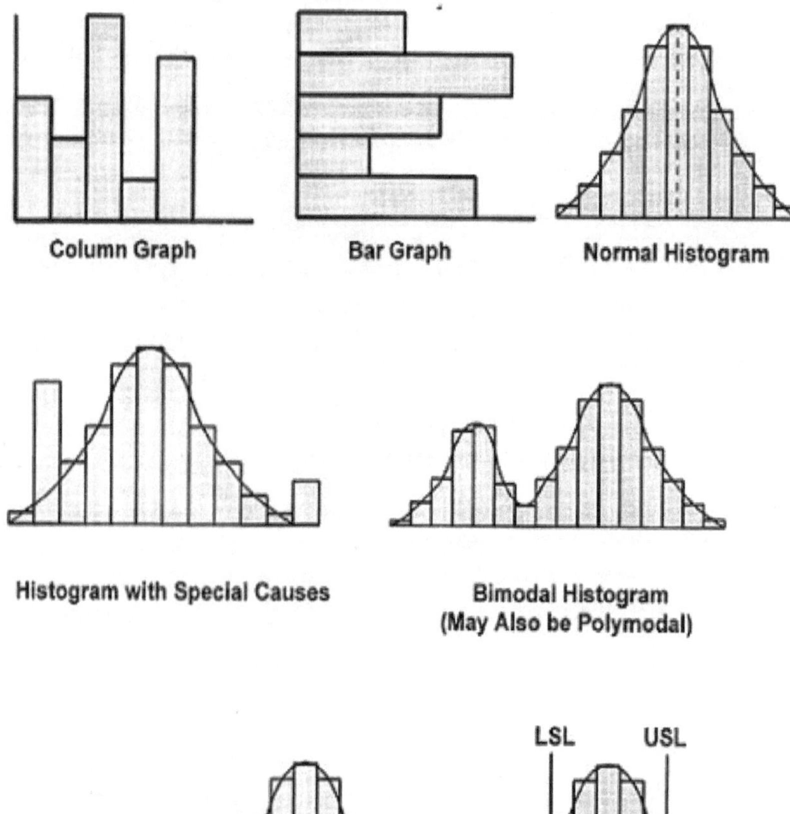

PARETO CHARTS

Definition—Pareto analysis is the process of ranking opportunities to determine which of many potential opportunities should be pursued first. It is also known as "separating the vital few from the trivial many."

Usage—Pareto analysis should be used at various stages in a quality improvement program to determine which step to take next. Pareto analysis is used to answer such questions as "What department should have the next SPC team?" or "On what type of defect should we concentrate our efforts?"

How to perform a Pareto analysis

1. Determine the classifications (Pareto categories) for the graph. If the desired information does not exist, obtain it by designing check sheets and logsheets.

2. Select a time interval for analysis. The interval should be long enough to be representative of typical performance.

3. Determine the total occurrences (i.e., cost, defect counts, etc.) for each category. Also determine the grand total. If there are several categories which account for only a small part of the total, group these into a category called "other."

4. Compute the percentage for each category by dividing the category total by the grand total and multiplying by 100.

5. Rank-order the categories from the largest total occurrences to the smallest.

6. Compute the "cumulative percentage" by adding the percentage for each category to that of any preceding categories.

7. Construct a chart with the left vertical axis scaled from 0 to at least the grand total. Put an appropriate label on the axis. Scale the right vertical axis from 0 to 100%, with 100% on the right side being the same height as the grand total on the left side.

8. Label the horizontal axis with the category names. The leftmost category should be the largest, second largest next, and so on.

9. Draw in bars representing the amount of each category The height of the bar is determined by the left vertical axis.

10. Draw a line that shows the cumulative percentage column of the Pareto analysis table. The cumulative percentage line is determined by the right vertical axis.

Example of Pareto analysis

The data in Table below has been recorded for boxes of apple arriving at Super Duper Market during August.

PROBLEM	APPLE LOST

Bruised	100
Undersized	87
Rotten	237
Rotten	9
Wrong variety	7
Wormy	3

The Pareto table for the data is given in the Table below.

RANK	PROBLEM	APPLE LOST	PERCENTAGE	CUMULATIVE PERCENTAGE
1	Rotten	235	53.29%	53.29%
2	Bruised	100	22.68%	75.97%
3	Undesired	87	19.73%	95.7%
4	Others	19	4.31%	100.01%

Note that, as often happens, the final percentage is slightly different than 100%. This is due to round-off error and is nothing to worry about. The finished diagram is shown in Figure below

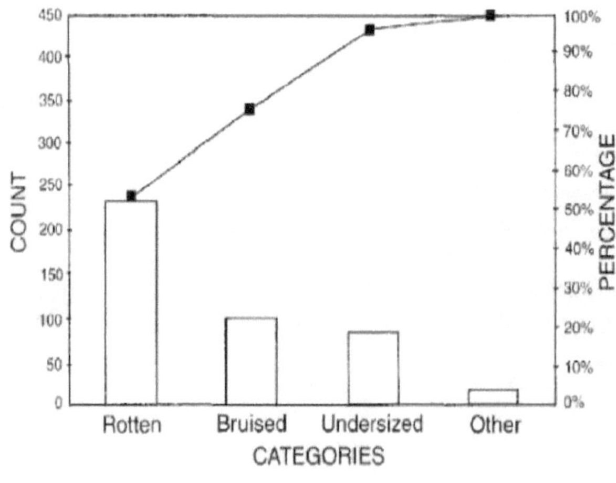

The completed Pareto diagram

SCATTER DIAGRAMS

Definition—A scatter diagram is a plot of one variable versus another. One variable is called the independent variable and it is usually shown on the horizontal (bottom) axis. The other variable is called the dependent variable and it is shown on the vertical (side) axis.

Usage—Scatter diagrams are used to evaluate cause and effect relationships. The assumption is that the independent variable is causing a change in the dependent variable. Scatter plots are used to answer such questions as "Does vendor As material machine better than vendor B's?" "Does the length of training have anything to do with the amount of scrap an operator makes?" and so on.

How to construct a scatter diagram

1. Gather several paired sets of observations, preferably 20 or more. A paired set is one where the dependent variable can be directly tied to the independent variable.

2. Find the largest and smallest independent variable and the largest and smallest dependent variable.

3. Construct the vertical and horizontal axes so that the smallest and largest values can be plotted. Plot the data by placing a mark at the point corresponding to each X-Y pair.Figure below shows the basic structure of a scatter diagram.If more than one classification is used, you may use different symbols to represent each group.

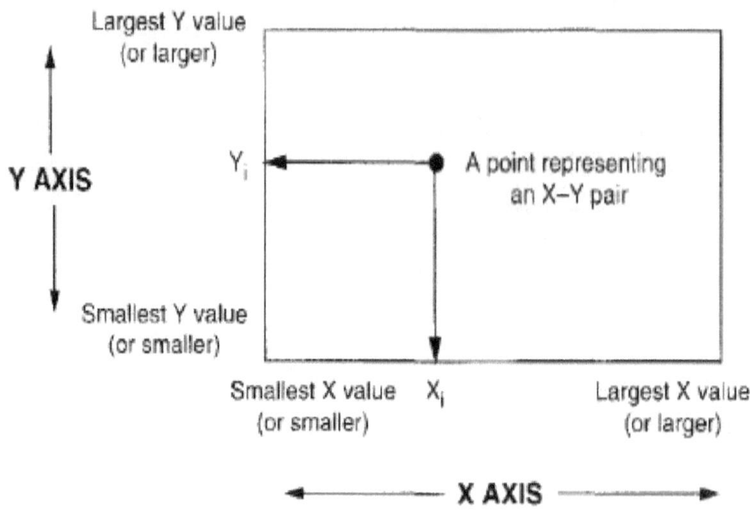

Example of a scatter diagram
The orchard manager has been keeping track of the weight of peaches on a day by day basis. The data are provided in Table below

NUMBER	DAYS ON TREES	WEIGHT (OUNCES)
1	75	4.5
2	76	4.5
3	77	4.4
4	78	4.6
5	79	5.0
6	80	4.8
7	80	4.9
8	81	5.1
9	82	5.2
10	82	5.2

11	83	5.5
12	84	5.4
13	85	5.5
14	85	5.5
15	86	5.6
16	87	5.7
17	88	5.8
18	89	5.8
19	90	6.0
20	90	6.1

1. Organize the data into X-Y pairs, as shown in Table V.4. The independent variable,X, is the number of days the fruit has been on the tree. The dependent variable, Y, is the weight of the peach.

2. Find the largest and smallest values for each data set. The largest and smallest values are as shown

VARIABLE	SMALLEST	LARGEST
Days on tree (X)	75	90
Weight of peach (Y)	4.4	6.1

3. Construct the axes. In this case, we need a horizontal axis that allows us to cover the range from 75 to 90 days. The vertical axis must cover the smallest of the small weights (4.4 ounces) to the largest of the weights (6.1 ounces). We will select values beyond these minimum requirements, because we want to estimate how long it will take for a peach to reach 6.5 ounces.

4. Plot the data. The completed scatter diagram is shown

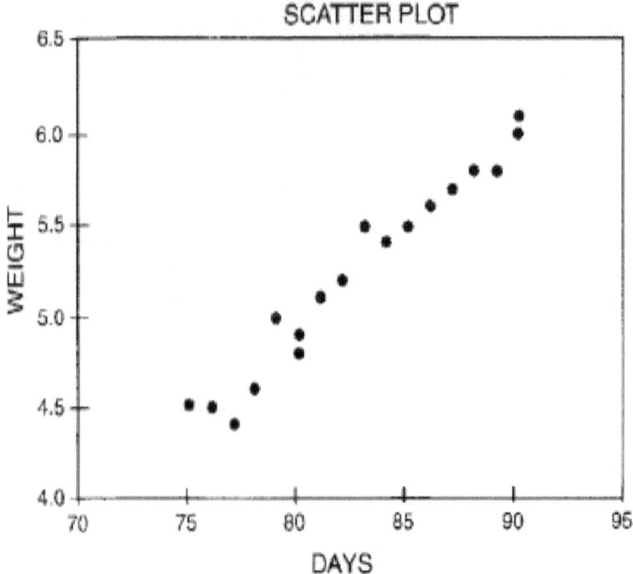

Using scatter diagrams

Scatter diagrams display different patterns that must be interpreted;Figure below provides a scatter diagram interpretation guide.

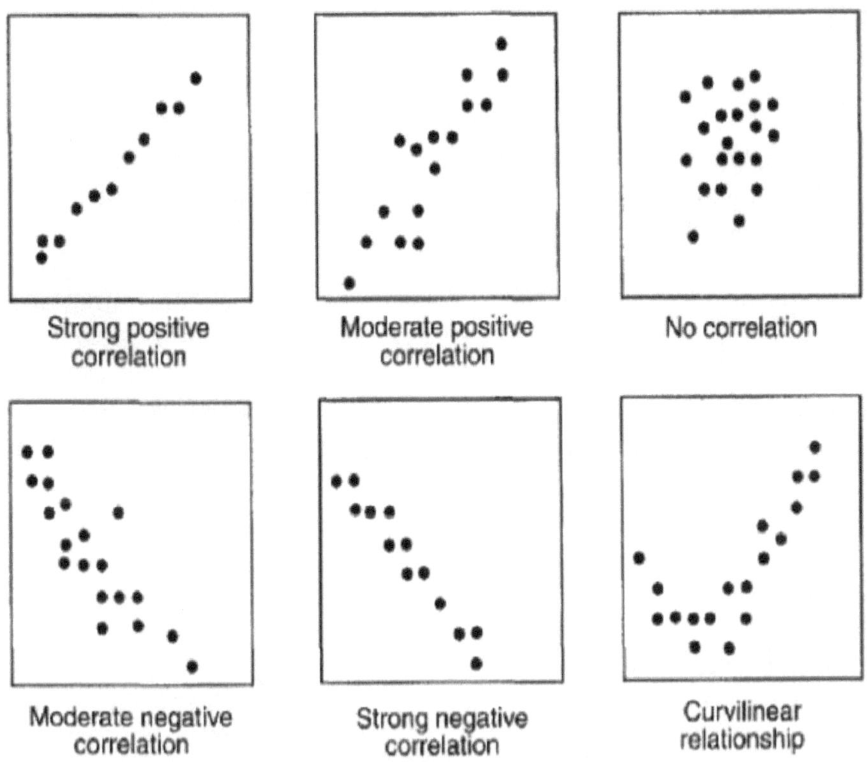

A Correlation Coefficient r can be calculated to determine the degree of association between the two variables

$$r = \frac{\sum\limits_{i=1}^{n}(X_i - \bar{X})(Y_i - \bar{Y})}{\sqrt{\left[\sum\limits_{i=1}^{n}(X_i - \bar{X})^2\right]\left[\sum\limits_{i=1}^{n}(Y_i - \bar{Y})^2\right]}}$$

Interpret the Relationship Between Two Variables

$r = -1.0$	strong negative	when X increases, Y decreases
$r = -0.5$	slight negative	when X increases, Y generally decreases
$r = 0$	no correlation	the two variables are independent
$r = +0.5$	slight positive	when X increases, Y generally increases
$r = +1.0$	strong positive	when X increases, Y increases

Be sure that the independent variable, X, is varied over a sufficiently large range. When X is changed only a small amount, you may not see a correlation with Y, even though the correlation really does exist.

If you make a prediction for Y, for an X value that lies outside of the range you tested, be advised that the prediction is highly questionable and should be tested thoroughly. Predicting a Y value beyond the X range actually tested is called extrapolation.

Watch for the effect of variables you didn't evaluate. Often, an uncontrolled variable will wipe out the effect of your X variable. It is also possible that an uncontrolled variable will be causing the effect and you will mistake the X variable you are controlling as the true cause. This problem is much less likely to occur if you choose X levels at random. An example of this is our peaches. It is possible that any number of variables changed steadily over the time period investigated. It is possible that these variables, and not the independent variable, are responsible for the weight gain (e.g., was fertilizer added periodically during the time period investigated?).

Beware of "happenstance" data! Happenstance data is data that was collected in the past for a purpose different than constructing a scatter diagram. Since little or no control was exercised over important variables, you may find nearly anything. Happenstance data should be used only to get ideas for further investigation, never for reaching final conclusions. One common problem with happenstance data is that the variable that is truly important is not recorded. For example, records might show a correlation between the defect rate and the shift. However, perhaps the real cause of defects is the ambient temperature, which also changes with the shift.

If there is more than one possible source for the dependent variable, try using different plotting symbols for each source. For example, if the orchard manager knew that some peaches were taken from trees near a busy highway, he could use a different symbol for those peaches. He might find an interaction, that is, perhaps the peaches from trees near the highway have a different growth rate than those from trees deep within the orchard. Although it is possible to do advanced analysis without plotting the scatter diagram, this is generally bad practice. This misses the enormous learning opportunity provided by the graphical analysis of the data.

FLOW CHARTS

A process flow chart is simply a tool that graphically shows the inputs, actions, and outputs of a given system. These terms are defined as follows:

Inputs—the factors of production: land, materials, labor, equipment, and management.

Actions—the way in which the inputs are combined and manipulated in order to add value. Actions include procedures, handling, storage, transportation, and processing.

Outputs—the products or services created by acting on the inputs. Outputs are delivered to the customer or other user. Outputs also include unplanned and undesirable results, such as scrap, rework, pollution, etc. Flow charts should contain these outputsas well.

EXERCISE 1
Flowchart for Cut Grass Process

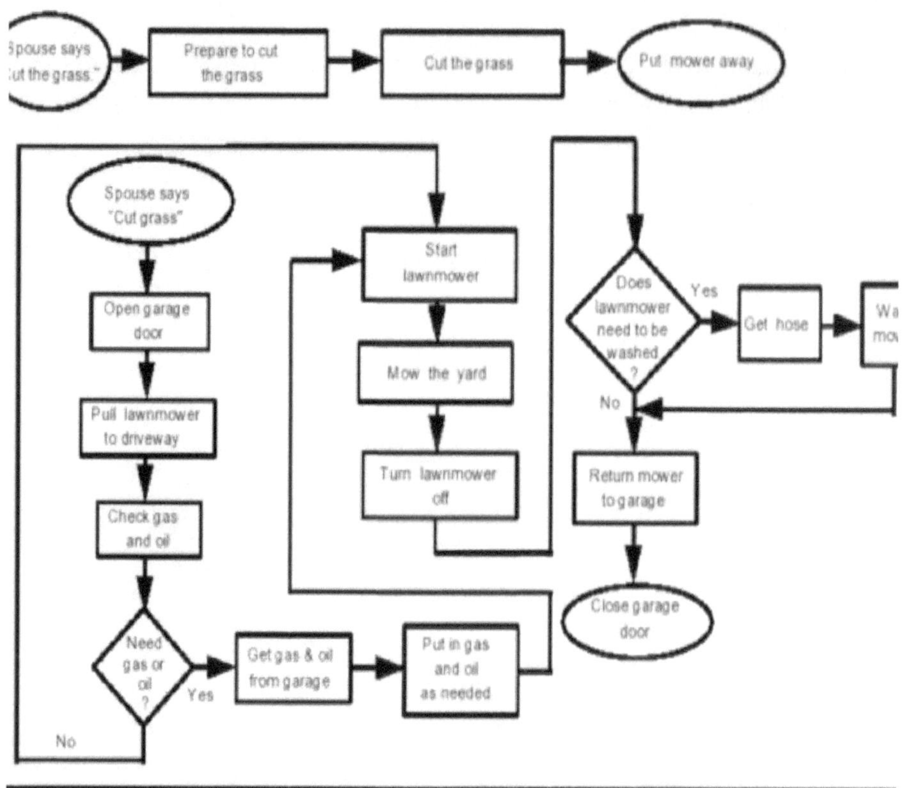

A flowchart or process map, is useful to people familiar with a process, as well as those that have a need to understand a process. A flow chart can depict the sequence of products, containers, paperwork, operator actions, or administrative procedures. A flow chart is often the starting point for process improvement by six sigma teams. Flow charts can be used to identify improvement opportunities as illustrated by the following sequence:

- Organize a team for the purpose of examining the process

- Construct a flow chart to represent each process step
- Discuss and analyze each step in detail
- Ask the key question, "Why do we do it this way?"
- Compare the actual process to an imagined "perfect" process
- Is there unnecessary complexity?
- Does duplication or redundancy exist?
- Are there control points to prevent errors or rejects? Should there be?
- Is this process being run the way it should?
- Improvement ideas may come from substantially different processes

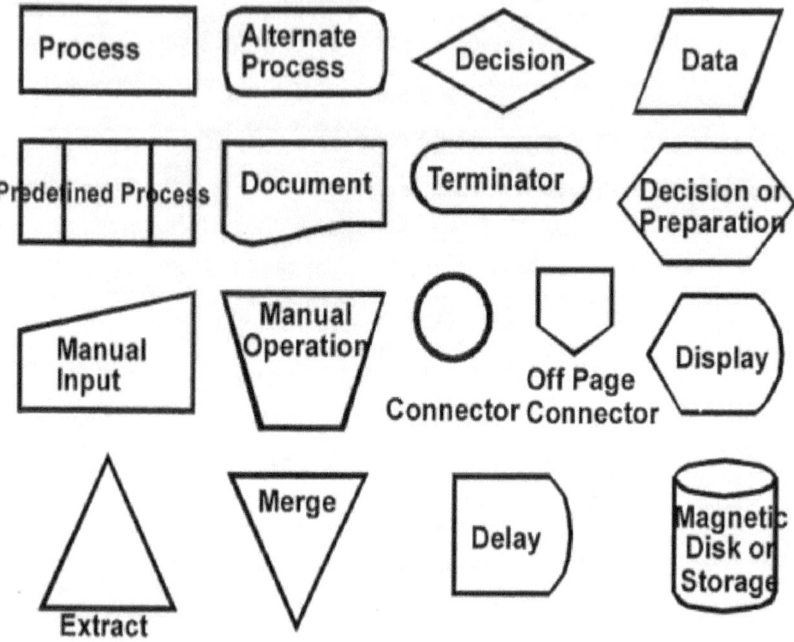

The flowchart in Figure below shows a high-level view of a process capability analysis. The flowchart can be made either more complex or less complex. As a rule of thumb, to paraphrase Albert Einstein, "Flow charts should be as simple as possible, but not simpler." The purpose of the flow chart is to help people understand the process and this is not accomplished with flow charts that are either too simple or too complex.

Flow charts shows unexpected complexity, problem areas, redundancy, unnecessary loops, and where simplification and standardization may be possible. It compares and contrasts the actual versus the ideal flow of a process to identify improvement opportunities. It allows a team to come to agreement on the steps of the process and to examine which activities may impact the process performance. It identifies locations where additional data can be collected and investigated. It serves as a training aid to understand the complete process

Steps in preparing the flowcharts

1. **Determine the frame or boundaries of the process**

    - Clearly define where the process under study starts (input) and ends (final output).

    - Team members should agree to the level of detail they must show on the Flowchart to clearly understand the process and identify problem areas.

    - The Flowchart can be a simple macro-flowchart showing only sufficient information to understand the general process flow, or it might be detailed to show every finite action and decision point. The team might start out with a macro flowchart and then add in detail later or only where it is needed.

2. **Determine the steps in the process**
    Brainstorm a list of all major activities, inputs, outputs, and decisions on a flipchart sheet from
    the beginning of the process to the end.

3. **Sequence the steps**
    Arrange the steps in the order they are carried out. Use Post-it® Notes so you can move them around. Don't draw in the arrows yet.Unless you are flowcharting a new process, sequence what is, not what should be or the ideal. This may be difficult at first but is necessary to see where the probable causes of the problems are in the process.

4. **Draw the Flowchart using the appropriate symbols.**

    - An oval is used to show the materials, information, or action (inputs) to start the process or to show the results at the end (output) of the process. A box or rectangle is used to show a task or activity performed in the process. Although multiple arrows may come into each box, usually only one output or arrow leaves each activity box.A diamond shows those points in the process where a yes/no question is being asked or a decision is required.
    A circle with either a letter or a number identifies a break in

the Flowchart and is continued elsewhere on the same page or another page.Arrows show the direction or flow of the process.

- Keep the Flowchart simple using the basic symbols. As your experience grows, use other, more graphic symbols to represent the steps. Other symbols sometimes used include:
    - A half or torn sheet of paper for a report completed and/or filed.
    - A can or computer tape wheel for data entry into a computer database.
    - A large "D" or half circle to identify places in the process where there is a delay or wait for further action.
- Be consistent in the level of detail shown.
    - A macro-level flowchart will show key action steps but no decision boxes.
    - An intermediate-level flowchart will show action and decision points.
    - A micro-level flowchart will show minute detail.
- Label each process step using words that are understandable to everyone.
- Add arrows to show the direction of the flow of steps in the process. Although it is not a rule, if you show all "yes" choices branching down and "no" choices branching to the left, it is easier to follow the process. Preferences and space will later dictate direction.
- Don't forget to identify your work. Include the title of your process, the date the diagram was made, and the names of the team members.

5. **Test the Flowchart for completeness**
    - Are the symbols used correctly?
    - Are the process steps (inputs, outputs, actions,decisions, waits/delays) identified clearly?

- Make sure every feedback loop is closed, i.e.,every path takes you either back to or ahead to another step.

- Check that every continuation point has a corresponding point elsewhere in the Flowchart or on another page of the Flowchart.

- There is usually only one output arrow out of an activity box. If there is more than one arrow, you may need a decision diamond.

- Validate the Flowchart with people who are not on the team and who carry out the process actions. Highlight additions or deletions they recommend. Bring these back to the team to discuss and incorporate into the final Flowchart.

6. **Finalize the Flowchart**

- Is this process being run the way it should be?

- Are people following the process as charted?

- Are there obvious complexities or redundancies that can be reduced or eliminated?

- How different is the current process from an ideal one? Draw an ideal Flowchart. Compare the two (current versus ideal) to identify discrepancies and opportunities for improvements.

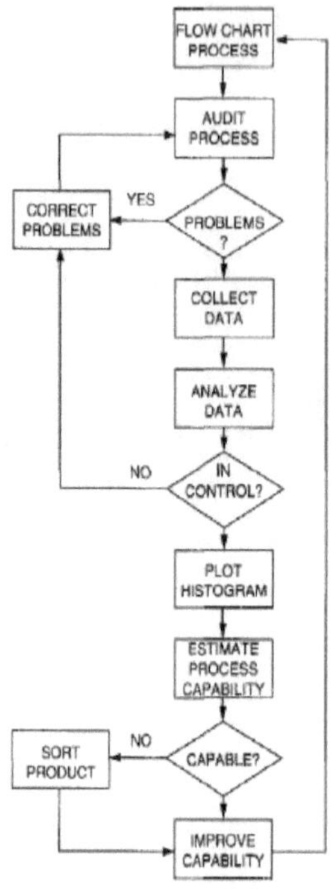

Flowchart of process capability analysis

Control Charts

Variation can be classified as common cause variation or special cause variation. Common cause variation is due to the natural variation of the process; that is, variation due to the way the process was designed. An example of common cause variation is the variation that might be seen by having several people working in the process. Each person might do things slightly differently. Special cause variation is variation that is due to assignable causes. An example of special cause variation is the variation that might result if someone untrained is allowed to work in the process. Special cause variation is variation that can be assigned a reason. The best tool to determine if the variation is common cause or special cause is the control chart. A control chart is a specialized run chart. The Y axis is the metric of interest and the X axis is time, or a factor that indicates time such as lot or run number. The difference between a run chart and a control chart is a control chart has three statistically calculated lines: a center line, an upper control limit, and a lower control limit. There are many types of control charts but generically these lines can be described as:

Center line = Mean of the metric of interest

Lower control limit = Mean of the metric − 3 * Standard Deviation of the metric

Upper control limit = Mean of the metric + 3 * Standard Deviation of the metric

Special cause variation is identified by points falling below the lower limit or above the upper limit, trends, runs or any unusual patterns. Any indication of a special cause should be investigated to see if the process has changed. Here is a control chart with all points in control.

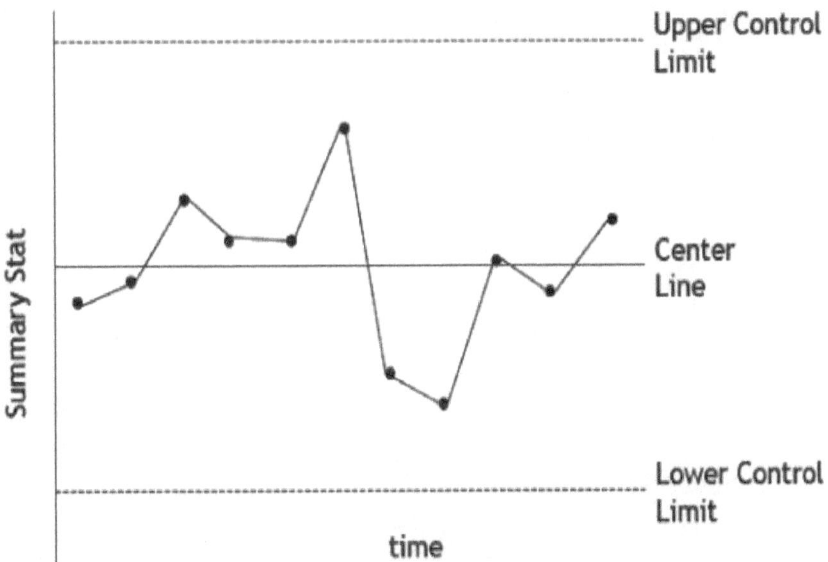

Example Control Chart

An important consideration when using a control chart is the subgroup size to use with the chart. In each time period, the data collected could be an individual value or a small sample, or subgroup. The determination of the size of the subgroup will be based on practical issues such as the cost of sampling, how quickly a change needs to be detected and the cost of investigating false alarms (false indications of instabilities).

To determine the subgroup size and frequency, consider the following:

- Determine the subgroup size so that the samples in the subgroup are produced under essentially the same conditions. The goal is for the effect of an assignable cause (x) to show up between subgroups, not within a subgroup. The variation within a subgroup should be due to non-assignable chance causes only.

- Ensure that the observations included in the subgroup are independent. Some processes may contain auto correlation as a natural function of the process (e.g., chemical processes). Autocorrelation is the dependence of a current data point on previous data points within a given single stream of data.

- Determine the frequency of sampling so that the control chart can detect any changes in the process over time. As an initial starting point, sample twice frequently as a change in the process could happen (e.g., if a change from shift-to-shift is possible, take two samples every shift.) Then, as the process proves to be stable over a period of time, consider reducing the frequency of sampling. Typically, for high-volume processes, taking small samples frequently is the best strategy.

Selecting the right control chart is based on whether the data to be plotted are continuous or discrete. If the data are continuous, two charts are suggested – one to monitor the location of the data and one to monitor the spread of the data. The typical charts for data collected in subgroups are an X-bar and an R chart. In other words, the two charts are a plot of the subgroup means and a plot of the ranges of the subgroups. If the data are collected one value at a time, typical charts are an Individuals chart and a Moving Range chart; in other words, a plot of the individual values and a plot of the moving ranges. For the moving range chart, the moving range is defined as the range between two adjacent data points.

If the data are discrete, one chart is usually plotted. The chart type is dependent on the nature of the data – whether the data are counts of defects or defective units. There are four traditional charts for discrete data. C and U charts are used for defects, where c is the count of defects and u is the average number of defects per unit. P charts and NP charts are used for defective units where p is the proportion of defective units and np is the count of defective units.

To generate a control chart, these steps should be followed:

1. Identify the process quality characteristic to be charted and the potential sources of variation of that characteristic.

2. Ensure that the data collected are appropriate for the construction of the control chart. Two common assumptions about the data are that they are independent and normally distributed. If these assumptions are not true, then a non-traditional control chart should be used.

3. Calculate the control limits.
   a. Initially, calculate the control limits using 25-30 data points. If that much data are not available, establish the limits with what is available. However, re-evaluate the limits as more data are obtained.
   b. When creating the control chart with these 25-30 data points, if any point is below the lower control limit or above the upper control limit, investigate to see if there was a special cause:

- If a special cause is found, eliminate that data point and recalculate the limits.

- If no special cause is found, keep the data point in the calculation of the limits.

- Document the details of the complete control plan for the process.

- Document the specific tests used to indicate out-of-control conditions and the associated corrective actions in the Out-of-Control Action Plan. This plan is described below.

- Decide when the control limits should be revised. Revise the limits if there has been a change in the process. Also, consider re-evaluating the limits after some time has pa

- **DRIVE** is an approach to problem solving and analysis that can be used as part of process improvement.

Define   the scope of the problem the criteria by which success will
be   measured and agree the deliverables and success factors

Review   the current situation, understand the background, identify and collect information,

including performance, identify problem areas, improvements and "quick wins"

Identify   improvements or solutions to the problem, required changes to enable and

sustain the improvements

Verify   check that the improvements will bring about benefits that meet the defined

success criteria, prioritise and pilot the improvements

Execute   plan the implementation of the solutions and improvements, agree and implement

them, plan a review, gather feedback and review

PROCESS   MAPPING

One of the initial steps to understand or improve a process is **Process Mapping**. By gathering information we can construct a "dynamic" model - a picture of the activities that take place in a process. Process maps are useful communication tools that help improvement teams understand the process and identify opportunities for improvement.

ICOR (inputs, outputs, controls and resources) is an internationally accepted process analysis methodology for process mapping. It allows processes to be broken down into simple, manageable and more easily understandable units. The maps define the inputs, outputs, controls and resources for both the high level process and the sub-processes.

Process mapping provides a common framework, discipline and language, allowing a systematic way of working. Complex interactions can be represented in a logical, highly visible and objective way. It defines where issues or "pinch points" exist and provides improvement teams with a common decision making framework.

To construct a process map:

- Brainstorm all activities that routinely occur within the scope of the process

- Group the activities into 4-6 key sub-processes

- Identify the sequence of events and links between the sub-processes

- Define as a high level process map and sub-process maps using ICOR

Process maps provide a dynamic view of how an organisation can deliver enhanced business value. *"What if"* scenarios can be quickly developed by comparing maps of the process *"As is"* with the process

Force Field Analysis is a technique for identifying forces which may help or hinder achieving a change or improvement. By assessing the forces that prevent making the change, plans can be developed to overcome them. It is also important to identify those forces that will help with the change. Once these forces have been identified and analysed, it is possible to determine if a proposed change is viable.

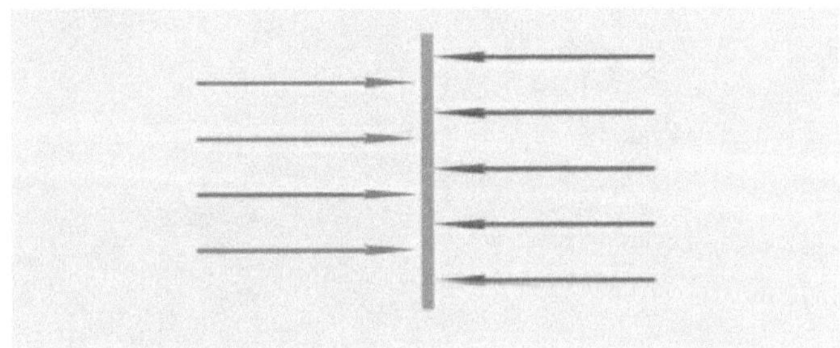

Brainstorming can be used in conjunction with the Cause and Effect tool. It is a group technique used to generate a large number of ideas quickly and may be used in a variety of situations. Each member of the group, in turn, can put forward an idea concerning the problem being considered. Wild ideas are welcomed and no criticism or evaluation occurs during brainstorming, all ideas being recorded for subsequent analysis. The process continues until no further ideas are forthcoming and increases the chance for originality and innovation. It can be used for:

- Identifying problem areas

- Identifying areas for improvement

- Designing solutions to problems

- Developing action plans

9 7 9 8 7 3 2 1 2 2 7 5 6